Annie's

Precuts Pizzazz

LEISURE ARTS, INC. • Maumelle, Arkansas

If you're one of those quilters who purchases precuts just because they're pretty and then later wonders what to do with them, well here are the patterns you need to turn them into gorgeous quilts, bed runners, place mats and so much more. *Precuts Pizzazz* contains 12 inspiring projects perfect for your stash of precuts. These beautiful and stylish quilt projects will delight you, and using precuts will cut down on your prep time. If you only have a limited amount of time dedicated to your quilting, this is the book for you.

ENJOY!

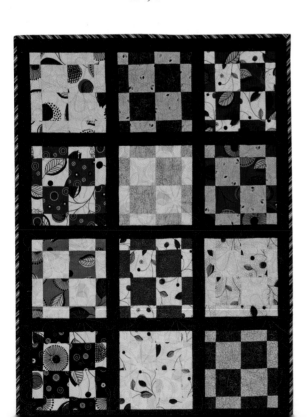

ANNIE'S STAFF
EDITOR **Carolyn S. Vagts**
CREATIVE DIRECTOR **Brad Snow**
PUBLISHING SERVICES DIRECTOR **Brenda Gallmeyer**
MANAGING EDITOR **Barb Sprunger**
TECHNICAL EDITOR **Angie Buckles**
COPY MANAGER **Corene Painter**
SENIOR COPY EDITOR **Emily Carter**
TECHNICAL ARTIST **Amanda Joseph**
SENIOR PRODUCTION ARTIST **Nicole Gage**
PRODUCTION ARTIST **Debera Kuntz**
PRODUCTION ASSISTANTS **Laurie Lehman, Marj Morgan, Judy Neuenschwander**
PHOTOGRAPHY SUPERVISOR **Tammy Christian**
PHOTOGRAPHY **Matthew Owen**
PHOTO STYLISTS **Tammy Liechty, Tammy Steiner**

CHIEF EXECUTIVE OFFICER **David McKee**
EXECUTIVE VICE PRESIDENT **Michele Fortune**

LEISURE ARTS STAFF
Editorial Staff
CREATIVE ART DIRECTOR **Katherine Laughlin**
PUBLICATIONS DIRECTOR **Leah Lampirez**
SPECIAL PROJECTS DIRECTOR **Susan Frantz Wiles**
PREPRESS TECHNICIAN **Stephanie Johnson**

Business Staff
PRESIDENT AND CHIEF EXECUTIVE OFFICER **Fred F. Pruss**
SENIOR VICE PRESIDENT OF OPERATIONS **Jim Dittrich**
VICE PRESIDENT OF RETAIL SALES **Martha Adams**
CHIEF FINANCIAL OFFICER **Tiffany P. Childers**
CONTROLLER **Teresa Eby**
INFORMATION TECHNOLOGY DIRECTOR **Brian Roden**
DIRECTOR OF E-COMMERCE **Mark Hawkins**
MANAGER OF E-COMMERCE **Robert Young**

ISBN-13/EAN: 978-1-4647-3337-6
UPC: 0-28906-06444-5

PROJECTS

Strip Dash Runner

Transform your bed or table in a weekend with this super-simple runner made out of sumptuous batik precuts. Precut strips make this a fast and easy weekend project.

Design by Tricia Lynn Maloney

Skill Level
Beginner

Finished Size
Runner Size: 90" x 22"

MATERIALS

- 45 precut 2½" x 15½" batik A strips
- ⅝ yard brown batik
- ¾ yard light blue-green batik
- Backing to size
- Batting to size
- Thread
- Basic sewing tools and supplies

CUTTING

From brown batik:
- Cut 6 (2¼" by fabric width) binding strips.

From light blue-green batik:
- Cut 3 (7½" by fabric width) strips.
  Subcut strips into 45 (2½" x 7½") B strips.

COMPLETING THE QUILT

1. Sew a B strip to an A strip to make an A-B unit as shown in Figure 1; press.

```
┌───┐
│ B │
├───┤
│   │
│ A │
│   │
└───┘
```

Figure 1

2. Repeat step 1 to make a total of 45 A-B units.
3. Select two different A-B units and join to make a strip unit, alternating the orientation of the pieces as shown in Figure 2. Repeat to make 22 strip units.

Make 22

Figure 2

4. Join two strip units to make an A-B quad unit as shown in Figure 3. Repeat to make 11 quad units.

Make 11

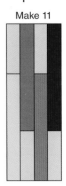

Figure 3

5. Join the quad units and add the extra A-B unit to one end to complete the pieced top.
6. Create a quilt sandwich referring to Quilting Basics on page 46.
7. Quilt as desired.
8. Bind referring to Quilting Basics on page 46 to finish. ●

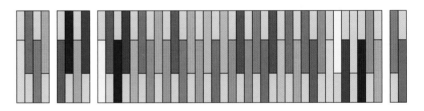

Strip Dash Runner
Assembly Diagram 90" x 22"

Reversible Around the World Runner

Reversing the placement of dark and light fabrics on the front and back yields a stylish runner that does double-duty. It's going to look great on your summer table.

Design by Connie Kauffman

Skill Level
Beginner

Finished Size
Runner Size: 40" x 22"

MATERIALS

- 1 Jelly Roll™ with red, cream and blue prints or
- 11 (2½" x 42") precut dark print strips
- 11 (2½" x 42") precut light print strips
- Backing to size
- Batting to size
- Thread
- Basic sewing tools and supplies

CUTTING

If using red, cream and blue prints, sort into light and dark prints.

From light precut strips:
- Cut 1 (2½" x 8") A rectangle.
- Cut 4 (2½") C squares.
- Cut 84 (2½" x 5") B rectangles.

From dark precut strips:
- Cut 1 (2½" x 8") A rectangle.
- Cut 4 (2½") C squares.
- Cut 84 (2½" x 5") B rectangles.

COMPLETING THE ROWS

1. Join one C, two B and four E pieces to make Dark Row 1 as shown in Figure 1; press seams away from B. Repeat to make two Dark Row 1s.
2. Join three B and four E pieces to make Dark Row 2 as shown in Figure 2; press seams toward E. Repeat to make two Dark Row 2s.

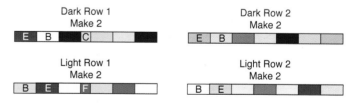

Dark Row 1
Make 2

Light Row 1
Make 2

Figure 1

Dark Row 2
Make 2

Light Row 2
Make 2

Figure 2

3. Join four each B and E pieces to make Dark Row 3 as shown in Figure 3; press seams toward E. Repeat to make two Dark Row 3s.

4. Join one F and four each B and E pieces to make Dark Row 4 referring to Figure 4; press seams toward E and F. Repeat to make two Dark Row 4s.

Figure 3   **Figure 4**

5. Join four B and five E pieces to make Dark Row 5 referring to Figure 5; press seams toward E. Repeat to make two Dark Row 5s.

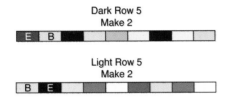

Figure 5

6. Join one D and four each B and E pieces to make Dark Row 6 as shown in Figure 6; press seams toward D and E.

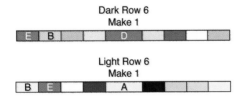

Figure 6

7. Join pieces as in steps 1–6 to make Light Rows 1–6, substituting E for B, B for E, C for F, F for C, and A for D referring to Figures 1–6 for positioning.

COMPLETING THE TOP

1. Center and join Dark Rows 1–6 and then add Dark Rows 5–1 to this section to complete the dark side of the runner; press seams in one direction.
2. Repeat step 1 with the Light Rows for the light side of the runner.
3. Measure and mark lines 3" from the last B piece on each end of each row of the dark runner top as shown in Figure 7.
4. Connect the marks to make a line for cutting as

shown in Figure 8; cut along the marked line to the center of Row 6. Repeat on each marked side to make a pleasing point on each end of the runner.

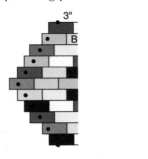

Figure 7   **Figure 8**

5. Use the trimmed dark side of the runner to trim the light side to match.

COMPLETING THE RUNNER

1. Layer batting, the light side of the runner right side up and dark side of the runner right side down; pin edges.
2. Sew all around, leaving a 4" opening along one side; trim batting and backing close to runner edges. Clip inner corners.
3. Turn right side out through opening; press edges flat.
4. Turn opening edges to the inside; hand-stitch closed.
5. Quilt as desired by hand or machine to finish. ●

Dark Reversible Around the World Runner
Placement Diagram 40" x 22"

Light Reversible Around the World Runner
Placement Diagram 40" x 22"

Windows

Simple piecing showcases the fabric choices in this easy-to-make bed runner and sham set.

Design by Sally Behrend

Skill Level
Beginner

Finished Size
Bed Runner Size: 91½" x 31½"
Pillow Sham Size: 31½" x 21½"
Block Size: 8½" x 8½" finished
Number of Blocks: 27 for bed runner; 12 for 2 shams

MATERIALS

- 8 fat quarters assorted dark-color prints
- 8 fat quarters assorted light-color prints
- 1 yard coordinating diagonal stripe
- 1⅞ yards muslin
- 3¼ yards black tonal
- Backing to size
- Batting to size
- Thread
- Basic sewing tools and supplies

Windows
8½" x 8½" Finished Block
Make 27 for bed runner
Make 12 for pillow shams

CUTTING

From assorted dark-color prints:
- Cut 3 (5¼" x 21") strips each fabric.
  Subcut 10 (5¼") A squares from each fabric.

From assorted light-color prints:
- Cut 3 (5¼" x 21") strips each fabric.
  Subcut 10 (5¼") B squares from each fabric.

From coordinating diagonal stripe:
- Cut 12 (2¼" by fabric width) binding strips.

From muslin:
- Cut 2 (29" by fabric width) rectangles.
  Subcut 2 (29" x 39") rectangles.

From black tonal:
- Cut 24 (2" by fabric width) strips.
  Subcut 24 (2" x 9") E strips, 10 (2" x 29") F strips, 8 (2" x 19") H strips and 4 (2" x 32") I strips.
- Cut 5 (2" by fabric width) G strips.
- Cut 2 (22" by fabric width) rectangles.
  Subcut 4 (20" x 22") J rectangles.

COMPLETING THE BLOCKS

1. To complete one Windows block, select two matching A and two matching B squares.
2. Sew an A square to a B square to make a row; press seam toward A. Repeat to make a second row.
3. Join the A-B rows to complete an A-B unit as shown in Figure 1; press seam to one side.
4. Place the A-B unit on a flat surface and trim a 1¾" C segment from opposite sides referring to Figure 2.

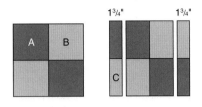

Figure 1   **Figure 2**

5. Reverse the C segments and sew back on the trimmed sides of the A-B unit as shown in Figure 3; press seams toward the C segments.
6. Turn the A-B-C unit with C segments at the top and bottom and trim a 1¾" D segment from opposite sides as shown in Figure 4.

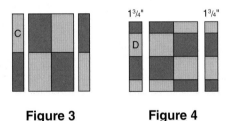

Figure 3   **Figure 4**

7. Reverse the D segments and sew back on the trimmed sides of the A-B-C unit as shown in Figure 5 to complete one Windows block; press seams toward the D segments.

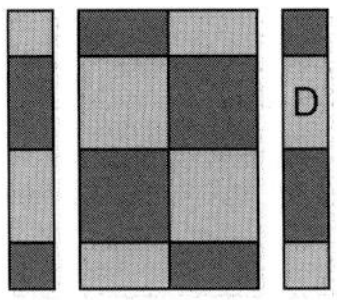

Figure 5

8. Repeat steps 1–7 to complete a total of 39 Windows blocks (27 for bed runner and 12 for two pillow shams).

COMPLETING THE BED RUNNER

1. Select 27 Windows blocks.
2. Arrange and join three Windows blocks with two E strips to make a block row as shown in Figure 6; press seams toward E. Repeat to make a total of nine block rows.
3. Join the block rows with the F strips, beginning and ending with an F strip; press seams toward F strips.
4. Join the G strips on the short ends to make a long strip; press seams open. Subcut strip into two 92" G strips.
5. Sew a G strip to opposite long sides of the pieced center to complete the runner top; press seam toward G strips.
6. Create a quilt sandwich referring to Quilting Basics on page 46.
7. Quilt as desired.
8. Bind referring to Quilting Basics on page 46 to finish.

Make 9

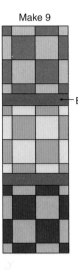

← E

Figure 6

COMPLETING THE PILLOW SHAMS

1. To complete one pillow sham, select six Windows blocks.
2. Join two Windows blocks with an E strip to make a block row referring to Figure 7; press seams toward E. Repeat to make a total of three block rows.
3. Join the three block rows with four H strips referring to the Assembly Diagram on page 13; press seams toward H strips.
4. Add an I strip to the top and bottom to complete one sham top, again referring to the Assembly Diagram; press seams toward I strips.
5. Sandwich a 39" x 29" batting rectangle between the sham top and a 39" x 29" muslin rectangle; pin or baste layers together to hold.
6. Quilt as desired by hand or machine. When quilting is complete, trim batting and muslin edges even with the edges of the sham top.
7. Turn ¼" to the wrong side on one 22" edge of two J rectangles and press; turn under the edge again, press and stitch to hem.

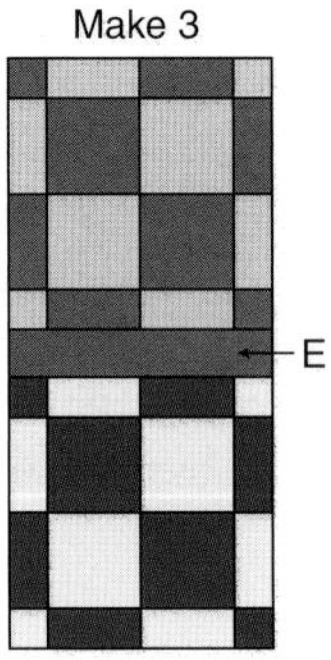

Make 3

← E

Figure 7

8. Place the hemmed J rectangles wrong sides together with the quilted top, matching raw edges and overlapping hemmed edges of J as shown in Figure 8; machine-baste to hold layers together.

Figure 8

9. Referring to Quilting Basics on page 46 and using the binding left over from the bed runner, bind edges to finish.

10. Repeat steps 1–9 to complete a second pillow sham. ●

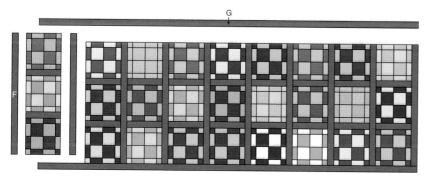

Windows Bed Runner
Assembly Diagram 91½" x 31½"

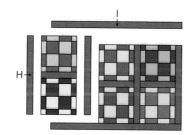

Windows Pillow Sham
Assembly Diagram 31½" x 21½"

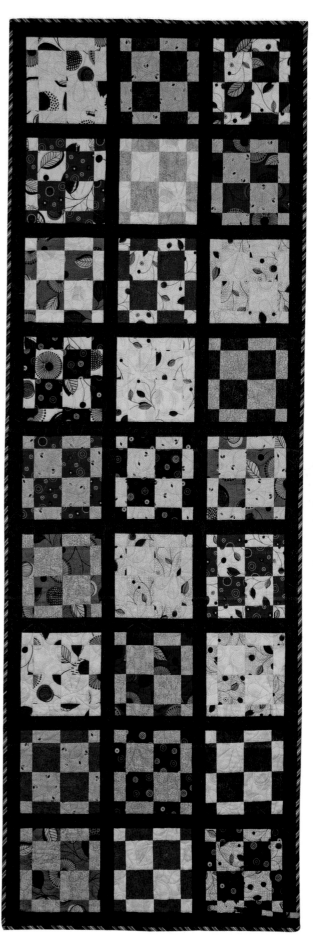

Summer Twist

A large, simple graphic quilt block makes short work of this breezy bed quilt.

Design by Tricia Lynn Maloney

Project Note: *Resist the notion to wash precuts! Washing might cause the fabric to fray, ravel or shrink, which means your 10" precut square probably won't be 10" square.*

Skill Level
Intermediate

Finished Size
Quilt Size: 67½" x 90"
Block Size: 22½" x 22½" finished
Number of Blocks: 12

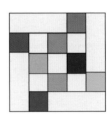

Twist Block
22¹/₂" x 22¹/₂" Finished Block
Make 12

MATERIALS

- 96 assorted 5" precut A squares
- ⅞ yard coordinating solid
- 3⅞ yards white solid
- Backing to size
- Batting to size
- Thread
- Basic sewing tools and supplies

CUTTING

From coordinating solid:
- Cut 8 (2¼" by fabric width) binding strips.

From white solid:
- Cut 8 (5" by fabric width) strips.
  Subcut into 60 (5") B squares.
- Cut 6 (14" by fabric width) strips.
  Subcut into 48 (5" x 14") C rectangles.

COMPLETING THE BLOCKS

1. Stitch a 5" precut A square between two B squares. Repeat to make two B-A-B rows.
2. Stitch a B square between two A charm squares.
3. Stitch the B-A-B row between two A-B-A rows referring to Figure 1 to make a Nine-Patch unit.

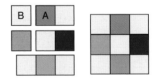

Figure 1

4. Stitch an A square to the end of a C rectangle (Figure 2). Repeat to make four C-A strips.

Figure 2

5. Position and stitch a C-A strip on the top of the Nine-Patch unit using a partial seam with the C end extending beyond the left side as shown in Figure 3. Press seam away from the Nine-Patch unit.

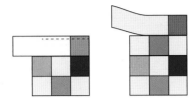

Figure 3

6. Stitch C-A strips to right side and then the bottom of the Nine-Patch unit referring to Figure 4. Always match A to a B square on the Nine-Patch unit and press seams away from the unit.

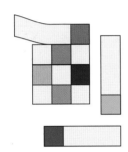

Figure 4

7. Stitch a C-A strip to the left side of the Nine-Patch unit, keeping the top C-A strip free of stitching (Figure 5). Press seam away from the Nine-Patch unit.

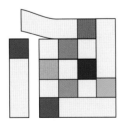

Figure 5

8. Complete the top strip seam as shown in Figure 6; press seam away from the Nine-Patch unit.

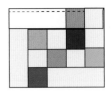

Figure 6

9. Repeat steps 1–8 to make 12 Twist blocks.

COMPLETING THE QUILT

1. Arrange and stitch Twist blocks in four rows of three blocks each referring to the Assembly Diagram.
2. Create a quilt sandwich referring to Quilting Basics on page 46.
3. Quilt as desired.
4. Bind referring to Quilting Basics on page 46 to finish. ●

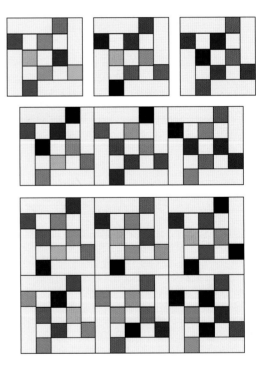

Summer Twist
Assembly Diagram 67½" x 90"

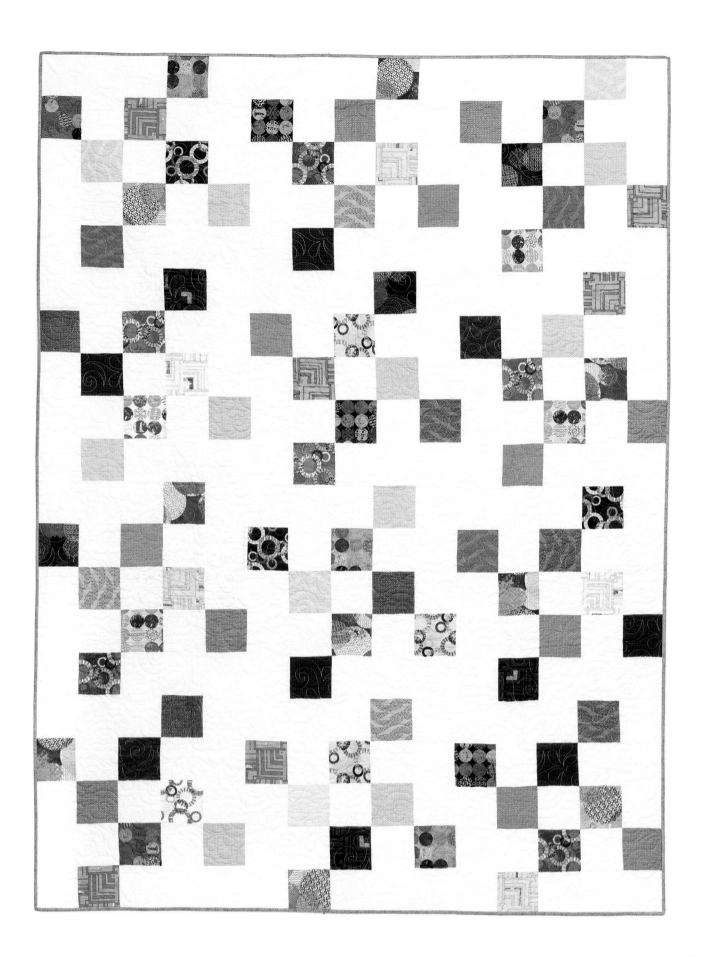

Progression

Precut 10" squares are perfect for this quilt, and cutting is kept to a minimum.

Design by Missy Shepler

Project Note: *This quilt is made up of three different Progression blocks. All blocks start the same way—with a large half-square triangle. Progression 2 and 3 blocks have additional strips. Careful, but not rigid, color placement helps to create a progression of color and value across the quilt. Refer to the Assembly Diagram for color/fabric placement in each block to create the color progression used in the sample quilt.*

Skill Level
Confident Beginner

Finished Size
Quilt Size: 59½" x 85"
Block Size: 8½" x 8½" finished
Number of Blocks: 70

MATERIALS

- 80 precut 10" batik B squares
- ⅔ yard blue batik
- 2⅞ yards white solid
- Backing to size
- Batting to size
- Thread
- Basic sewing tools and supplies

CUTTING

From blue batik:
- Cut 8 (2¼" by fabric width) binding strips.

From white solid:
- Cut 9 (10" by fabric width) strips. Subcut into 35 (10") A squares.

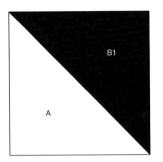

Progression 1
8½" x 8½" Finished Block
Make 30

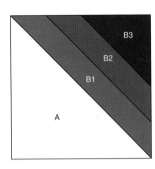

Progression 2
8½" x 8½" Finished Block
Make 20

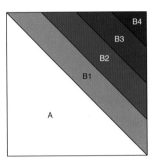

Progression 3
8½" x 8½" Finished Block
Make 20

COMPLETING THE BLOCKS

1. Draw a line from corner to corner on the wrong side of each A square.
2. Place a B square right sides together with an A square matching raw edges. Stitch ¼" on each side of the marked line. Cut apart on the marked line to make two A-B1 block units as shown in Figure 1; press seams open. Repeat with all A and B squares to make a total of 70 A-B1 block units.

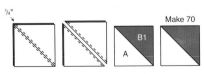

Figure 1

3. Select 30 A-B1 block units for Progression 1 blocks; trim each block to 9" square using the seam between the A and B pieces as a centering guide as shown in Figure 2.

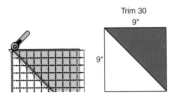

Figure 2

4. From the remaining 40 A-B1 block units, select a unit and draw a line 1½" from the seam line on the wrong side of B1 as shown in Figure 3.

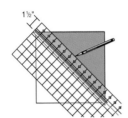

Figure 3

5. Place a B square right sides together with the marked block and with the A-B1 unit on top, stitch on the marked line to create the B2 strip as shown in Figure 4; trim seam allowance to ¼", press B2 to the right side and press seam open. *Note: To create the color progression in the blocks, pay careful attention to the fabrics used as B2 strips in each block. Refer to color photo of sample quilt for color placement.*

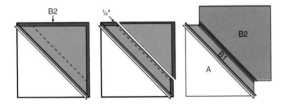

Figure 4

6. Draw a line on the wrong side of the B2 piece 1½" from the B1-B2 seam line as shown in Figure 5; place a B square right sides together with the A-B1-B2 unit and stitch on the marked line to

create the B3 strip; trim seam allowance to ¼", press B3 to the right side and press seam open as shown in Figure 6.

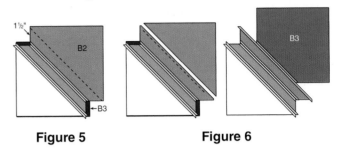

Figure 5   **Figure 6**

7. Using the diagonal seam between the A and B1 piece as the centering guide, trim the stitched unit to 9" square to complete a Progression 2 block as shown in Figure 7.

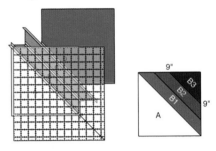

Figure 7

8. Repeat steps 4–7 to complete a total of 40 A-B1-B2-B3 block units; set aside 20 units for Progression 2 blocks.

9. Select one of the remaining A-B1-B2-B3 block units and mark a line 1½" from the B3 stitching line as in step 4. Repeat steps 5 and 7 to add a B4 strip to complete one Progression 3 block referring to Figure 8.

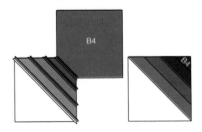

Figure 8

10. Repeat step 9 to complete a total of 20 Progression 3 blocks.

COMPLETING THE QUILT

1. Arrange and join 10 Progression 3 blocks to make the vertical row 1 referring to the Assembly Diagram; press seams open.

2. Repeat step 1 with 10 more Progression 3 blocks arranging blocks as shown in the Assembly Diagram to complete the vertical row 2; press seams open.

3. Complete vertical rows 3 and 4 with Progression 2 blocks and vertical rows 5, 6 and 7 with Progression 1 blocks to complete the rows.

4. Arrange and join the rows referring to the Assembly Diagram to complete the quilt top; press.

5. Create a quilt sandwich referring to Quilting Basics on page 46.

6. Quilt as desired.

7. Bind referring to Quilting Basics on page 46 to finish. ●

Tip

When using trimmed fabric pieces for strips, make sure that the angled edge of the trimming overlaps the marked line by at least ¼". Check the size of the trimmed fabrics before adding a new strip to a block. With block and strip right sides together, hold fabric together along the seam line. Flip fabrics right side up to ensure that the new strip is large enough to cover the strip area plus the seam allowances.

Progression
Assembly Diagram 59½" x 85"

Cracked Ice

Blue 10" squares and matching yardage were used to make this quilt. Imagine your fabric choice in this pattern.

Design by Connie Kauffman

Project Note: *If using precut 10" squares in packages with coordinating purchased border fabrics and fabric for C strips, remove any squares that match the fabric used for the C strips as the pattern will not show if C is the same fabric as any of the A or B triangles.*

Skill Level
Confident Beginner

Finished Size
Quilt Size: 83" x 92"
Block Size: 9" x 9" finished
Number of Blocks: 42

Cracked Ice
9" x 9" Finished Block
Make 42

MATERIALS

- 52 coordinating 10" precut squares
- ½ yard blue tonal 1
- ½ yard blue tonal 2
- 1⅔ yards blue print
- 2 yards dark blue print
- Backing to size
- Batting to size
- Thread
- Large square ruler
- Spray starch and cotton swab or brush (optional)
- Basic sewing tools and supplies

CUTTING

From precut squares:
- Select 10 (10") precut squares and cut 40 (2¼" x 10") binding strips.

From blue tonal 1:
- Cut 3 (3½" by fabric width) F1/G1 strips.

From blue tonal 2:
- Cut 3 (3½" by fabric width) F2/G2 strips.

From blue print:
- Cut 14 (1" by fabric width) E strips.
- Cut 7 (5" by fabric width) H strips.

From dark blue print:
- Cut 8 (7½" by fabric width) I/J strips.

COMPLETING THE BLOCKS

1. Stack four or five squares right side up and cut in half on one diagonal to make two triangles from each fabric; leave in stacks as cut.
2. Measure 3½" from the square corner on one stack of triangles and cut to make A and B pieces as shown in Figure 1; leave pieces as cut.
3. Measure down 5½" from the square corner of the second stack of triangles and cut to make C and D pieces referring to Figure 2. Leave pieces as cut.

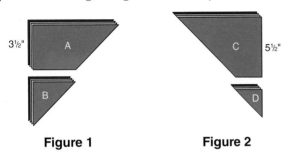

Figure 1   **Figure 2**

4. Repeat steps 1–3 with remaining squares. Place all A pieces in one stack; repeat with B, C and D pieces.
5. Mix up the pieces within each stack as shown in Figure 3 so that the same fabric pieces will not be sewn together.
6. Select the top A and B pieces and sew an E strip to the cut edge of the A piece as shown in Figure 4; press seam toward E.

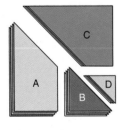

Figure 3   **Figure 4**

7. Add the B piece to the E side of the unit and press seam toward B as shown in Figure 5.
8. Trim the E strip even with the angle of pieces A and B to complete the A-E-B unit as shown in Figure 6.

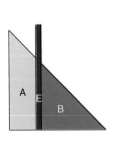
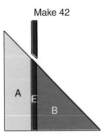

Make 42

Figure 5   **Figure 6**

9. Repeat steps 6–8 to make a total of 42 A-E-B units.
10. Repeat steps 6–8 with C and D pieces and E strips to make 42 C-E-D units as shown in Figure 7.

Make 42

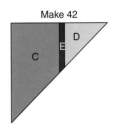

Figure 7

11. Select one each A-E-B and C-E-D unit and join to complete one Cracked Ice block as shown in Figure 8. *Note: When sewing bias edges together, apply spray starch to the bias edges to help secure these edges during stitching. Spray a little of the starch into a small paper cup and use a brush or cotton swab to apply the starch to the bias edges.*
12. Square up the block to 9½" square, centering the diagonal seam when trimming as shown in Figure 9.

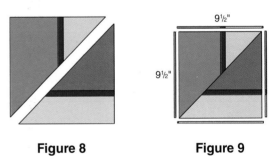

Figure 8   **Figure 9**

13. Repeat steps 11 and 12 to complete a total of 42 Cracked Ice blocks.

COMPLETING THE QUILT

1. Arrange and join the Cracked Ice blocks in seven rows of six blocks each, turning blocks as needed in rows referring to the Assembly Diagram for positioning of blocks; press. *Note: Try to arrange blocks so the same fabric is not side by side.*
2. Join the rows referring to the Assembly Diagram to complete the pieced center; press.
3. Join the F1/G1 strips on short ends to make a long strip; press. Subcut strips into one 3½" x 63½" F1 strip and one 3½" x 60½" G1 strip.

4. Repeat step 3 with F2/G2 strips.
5. Sew F1 to one side and F2 to the opposite side and G1 and G2 strips to the top and bottom of the pieced center referring again to the Assembly Diagram; press seams toward strips.
6. Join the H strips on short ends to make a long strip; press. Subcut strip into four 5" x 69½" H strips.
7. Sew an H strip to opposite sides and then to the top and bottom of the pieced center; press seams toward strips.
8. Join the I/J strips on short ends to make a long strip; press. Subcut strip into two 6½" x 78½" I strips and two 6½" x 83½" J strips.
9. Sew I strips to opposite sides and J strips to the top and bottom of the pieced center to complete the pieced top; press seams toward I and J strips.
10. Create a quilt sandwich referring to Quilting Basics on page 46.
11. Quilt as desired.
12. Bind referring to Quilting Basics on page 46 to finish. ●

Cracked Ice
Assembly Diagram 83" x 92"

Trellised Garden

This garden will last all year long. A little effort, a few fat quarters and some white fabric will produce this garden in a weekend.

Design by Chris Malone

Skill Level
Confident Beginner

Finished Size
Quilt Size: 85" x 102"
Block Size: 8½" x 8½" finished
Number of Blocks: 120

MATERIALS

- 30 fat quarters assorted coordinating pastel prints in rose, lavender, yellow, green and blue
- 1 yard green dot
- 2⅛ yards white tonal
- Backing to size
- Batting to size
- Thread
- 9" or larger square ruler
- Basic sewing tools and supplies

CUTTING

From each assorted pastel print fat quarter:
- Cut 4 (9") squares to total 120 squares.
  Subcut each square in half on 1 diagonal to make 240 A triangles.

From green dot:
- Cut 10 (2¼" by fabric width) strips for binding.

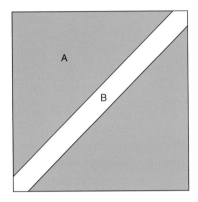

Trellis
8½" x 8½" Finished Block
Make 120

From white tonal:
- Cut 5 (13" by fabric width) strips.
  Subcut strips into 120 (1½" x 13") B strips.

COMPLETING THE BLOCKS

1. Select two same-fabric A triangles and one B strip to complete one Trellis block.
2. Fold each of the selected A triangles in half on the long side on the cut edge and crease to mark the centers as shown in Figure 1.

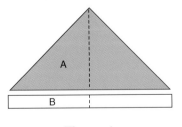

Figure 1

3. Fold the B strip to mark the center, again referring to Figure 1.

4. Matching center marks, sew an A triangle to opposite sides of B as shown in Figure 2.

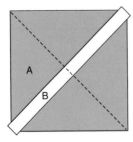

Figure 2

5. Place the block on a cutting mat and align the 45-degree line on the square ruler with the center of the white strip and trim the block to 9" x 9" to complete as shown in Figure 3.

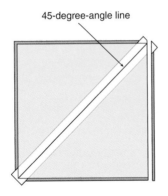

45-degree-angle line

Figure 3

6. Repeat steps 1–5 to complete a total of 120 Trellis blocks.

COMPLETING THE QUILT

1. Arrange and join 10 Trellis blocks to make a row referring to Figure 4; press seams to the right. Repeat to make a total of 12 rows.

Make 12

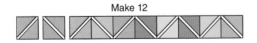

Figure 4

2. Arrange and join the rows to form the trellis design to complete the quilt top referring to the Assembly Diagram for positioning of rows; press seams in one direction.
3. Create a quilt sandwich referring to Quilting Basics on page 46.
4. Quilt as desired.
5. Bind referring to Quilting Basics on page 46 to finish. ●

Trellised Garden
Assembly Diagram 85" x 102"

Bird's Eye View

Piece 2½" precut strips together to create brilliant sashing between simply charming piecing. This quilt would work with any fabric.

Design by Gina Gempesaw

Skill Level
Confident Beginner

Finished Size
Quilt Size: 72" x 89½"
Block Size: 10" x 10" finished
Number of Blocks: 32

MATERIALS

- 32 (5") precut squares
- 40 (2½" by fabric width) precut strips
- 3⅞ yards white solid
- Backing to size
- Batting to size
- Thread
- Basic sewing tools and supplies

CUTTING

From precut strips:

- Cut a total of 130 (2½" x 10") F rectangles and 10 (2½" x 5¼") G rectangles.

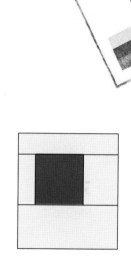

Bird's Eye View
10" x 10" Finished Block
Make 32

From white solid:

- Cut 5 (5" by fabric width) strips.
  Subcut strips into 32 each 4" x 5" A rectangles and 2" x 5" B rectangles.
- Cut 5 (10" by fabric width) strips.
  Subcut strips into 32 each 4" x 10" C rectangles and 2" x 10" D rectangles.
- Cut 2 (5¼" by fabric width) strips.
  Subcut 8 (5¼" x 10") E rectangles.
- Cut 16 (2½" by fabric width) strips.
  Set aside 8 strips for H/I and 8 strips for binding.

COMPLETING THE BLOCKS

1. Stitch a precut 5" square between B and A referring to Figure 1; press seams toward the precut square.

Figure 1

2. Stitch D to top and C to bottom of B-A-precut square unit and press seams toward C and D referring to Figure 2.

Figure 2

3. Repeat steps 1 and 2 to make 32 Bird's Eye blocks referring to the block diagram.

COMPLETING THE QUILT CENTER

1. Select and join eight assorted blocks and two E rectangles as shown in Figure 3 for block orientation. Repeat to make four block rows.

Make 4

Figure 3

2. Select and join nine F rectangles on short ends (Figure 4); press seams in one direction. Repeat to make 10 F strips.

F Strip
Make 10

F-G Strips
Make 5

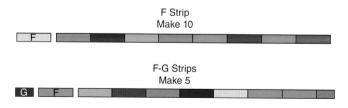

Figure 4

3. Select and join eight F rectangles and two G rectangles on short ends referring again to Figure 4; press seams in one direction. Repeat to make five F-G strips.

4. Stitch an F-G strip between two F strips referring to Figure 5; press seams toward F-G strips. Repeat to make five sashing units.

Sashing Unit
Make 5

Figure 5

5. Stitch the four block rows alternately with the five sashing units referring to the Assembly Diagram. Press seams away from the block rows.

COMPLETING THE QUILT

1. Join the H/I strips together on short ends to make one long strip; press seams in one direction.
2. Cut the long strip into two each 2½" x 85½" H and 2½" x 72½" I borders. Stitch H to both sides and I to top and bottom of quilt.
3. Create a quilt sandwich referring to Quilting Basics on page 46.
4. Quilt as desired.
5. Bind referring to Quilting Basics on page 46 to finish. ●

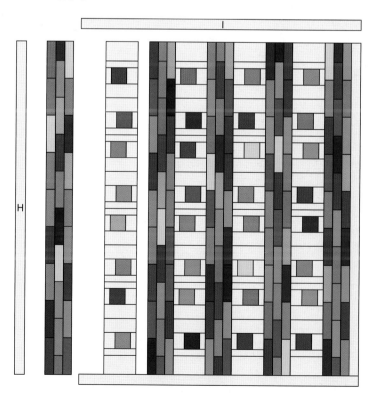

Bird's Eye View
Assembly Diagram 72" x 89½"

Apple of My Eye

Fat quarters, or a collection of 10" squares, could easily make this quilt.

Design by Wendy Sheppard

Skill Level
Confident Beginner

Finished Size
Quilt Size: 50" x 50"
Block Size: 2" x 2" finished
Number of Blocks: 56

MATERIALS

- 5 fat quarters bright pastel prints
- 5 fat quarters coordinating pastel tonals
- ½ yard pastel floral print
- 1¼ yards apple print
- 1⅜ yards white solid
- Backing to size
- Batting to size
- Thread
- Basic sewing tools and supplies

CUTTING

From bright pastel prints:
- Cut a total of 49 (3½") E squares.

From coordinating pastel tonals:
- Cut a total of 64 (2½") B squares.

From pastel floral print:
- Cut 5 (2½" by fabric width) H/I strips.

From apple print:
- Cut 5 (3½" by fabric width) L/M strips.
- Cut 6 (2¼ by fabric width) binding strips.

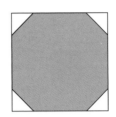

Snowball Block
2" x 2" Finished Block
Make 56

From white solid:
- Cut 9 (2½" by fabric width) strips.
  Subcut 104 (2½" x 3½") C rectangles.
- Cut 6 (1" by fabric width) strips.
  Subcut 224 (1") A squares.
- Cut 9 (1¼" by fabric width) strips.
  Subcut 2 each 1¼" x 37½" G and 1¼" x 39" F border strips. Set aside remaining strips for J and K borders.

COMPLETING THE BLOCKS

1. Draw diagonal lines on wrong side of all A squares.
2. Position A in one corner of B referring to Figure 1 and stitch on marked line. Trim seam to ¼" and press A away from B. Repeat on all four corners of B.

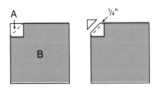

Figure 1

3. Repeat step 2 to make 64 Snowball blocks.

COMPLETING THE QUILT CENTER

1. Select, arrange as desired and join seven Snowball blocks and eight C rectangles alternately as shown in Figure 2 to make Row 1. Press seams toward C. Make a total of eight rows. **Note:** *The designer chose to make two each pink, yellow and blue rows and two red and green rows as seen in the Assembly Diagram.*

Row 1
Make 8

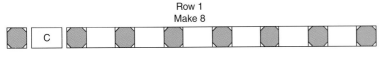

Figure 2

2. Select, arrange as desired and join seven assorted E squares and eight D rectangles alternately referring to Figure 3 to make Row 2. Press seams toward C. Make a total of seven rows.

Row 2
Make 7

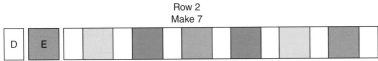

Figure 3

3. Join rows along length alternately beginning and ending with Row 1 and referring to the Assembly Diagram. Press seams in one direction. **Note:** *The Assembly Diagram shows the designer's row placement. If you do not arrange Row 2 like the designer your quilt center will look different.*

COMPLETING THE QUILT

1. Stitch G strips to the quilt center sides; press seam toward G. Stitch F strips to quilt center top and bottom; press seams toward F.
2. Stitch H/I strips together on short ends to make one long strip; press seams in one direction. Cut strip into two each 2½" x 39" H side borders and 2½" x 43" I top/bottom borders.

3. Stitch H to both sides of quilt top and I to top and bottom; press seams toward H and I.
4. Stitch the J/K strips together on short ends to make one long strip; press seams in one direction. Cut strip into two each 1¼" x 43" J side borders and 1¼" x 44½" K top/bottom borders.
5. Stitch J to both sides of quilt top and K to top and bottom; press seams toward J and K.
6. Stitch L/M strips together on short ends to make one long strip; press seams in one direction. Cut strip into two each 3½" x 44½" L side borders and 3½" x 50½" M top/bottom borders.
7. Stitch L to both sides of quilt top and M to top and bottom; press seams toward L and M.
8. Create a quilt sandwich referring to Quilting Basics on page 46.
9. Quilt as desired.
10. Bind referring to Quilting Basics on page 46 to finish. ●

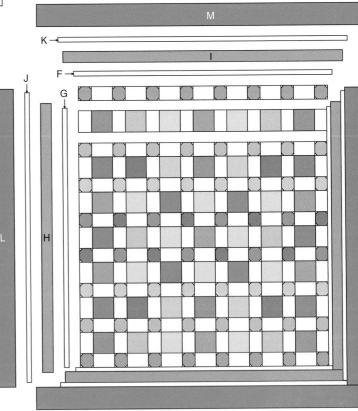

Apple of My Eye
Assembly Diagram 50" x 50"

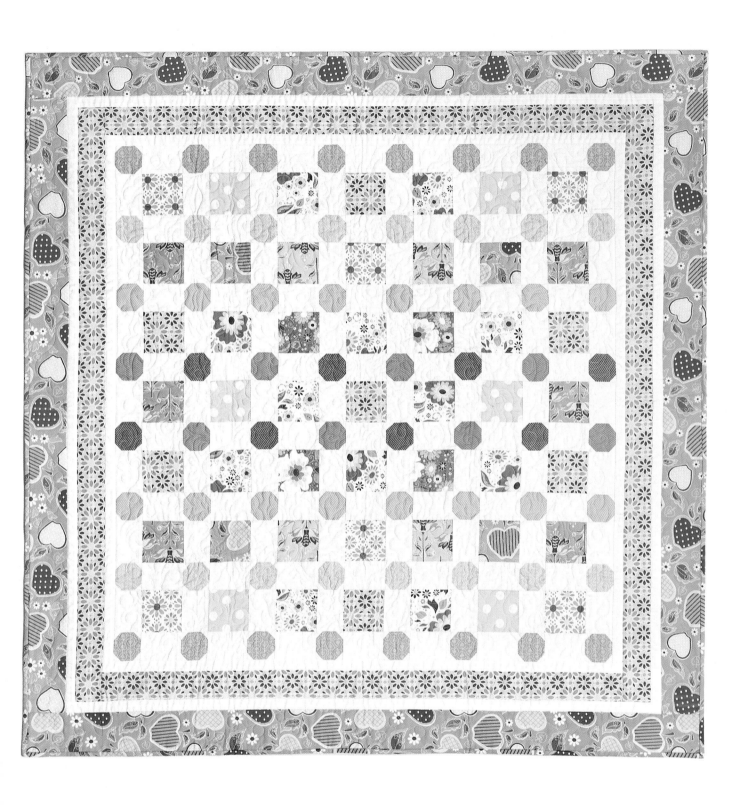

Square It Up

This quilt provides a great way to play with a scrappy layout. Just pick a strip and go with it!

Design by Chris Malone

Skill Level
Confident Beginner

Finished Size
Quilt Size: 80" x 90"
Block Size: 10" x 10" finished
Number of Blocks: 72

MATERIALS

- 117 precut 2½" by fabric width strips assorted blue, green and purple prints in light, medium and dark values
- Backing to size
- Batting to size
- Thread
- Basic sewing tools and supplies

CUTTING
Sort assorted blue, green and purple print strips into dark and light groups. Set aside 9 strips for binding. The remaining assortments of dark and light strips should be equal in number.

From dark strips:
- Cut 36 (2½") A squares for block centers.
- From the same print, cut 36 sets of 2 (2½") B squares and 2 (2½" x 6½") C strips.
- From the same print, cut 36 sets of 2 (2½" x 6½") D and 2 (2½" x 10½") E strips.

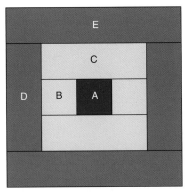

Dark-Bordered Square
10" x 10" Finished Block
Make 36

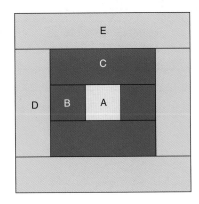

Light-Bordered Square
10" x 10" Finished Block
Make 36

Note: *For maximum yield when cutting these sets, from a single strip cut two D strips and two E strips; reserve remaining scrap. Cut 4 (2½") B squares and 4 C strips from a single strip; reserve scrap. Cut the A squares from the reserved scraps.*

From light strips:
- Repeat dark strip cutting instructions.

COMPLETING THE BLOCKS

1. To complete a Dark-Bordered Square block, select a matching set of light B squares and C strips, a matching set of dark D and E strips, and a different-fabric dark A square.

2. Sew a B square to opposite sides of the A square; press seams toward B. Sew a C strip to the top and bottom of the A-B unit as shown in Figure 1; press seams toward C.

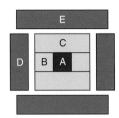

Figure 1

3. Sew a D strip to the B sides of the A-B-C unit and an E strip to the C sides to complete one Dark-Bordered Square block, again referring to Figure 1.

4. Repeat steps 1–3 to complete a total of 36 Dark-Bordered Square blocks.

5. To complete a Light-Bordered Square block, select a matching set of dark B squares and C strips, a matching set of light D and E strips, and a different-fabric light A square.

6. Repeat steps 2 and 3 to complete one Light-Bordered Square block referring to Figure 2.

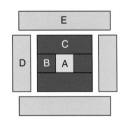

Figure 2

7. Repeat steps 5 and 6 to complete a total of 36 Light-Bordered Square blocks.

COMPLETING THE QUILT

1. Select and join four each Light- and Dark-Bordered Square blocks, turning every other block referring to Figure 3 to make a row; press seams toward Dark-Bordered Square blocks. Repeat to make nine rows.

Make 9

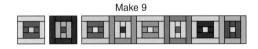

Figure 3

2. Arrange and join the rows, turning every other row referring to the Assembly Diagram, to complete the pieced top; press seams in one direction.

3. Create a quilt sandwich referring to Quilting Basics on page 46.

4. Quilt as desired.

5. Bind referring to Quilting Basics on page 46 to finish. ●

Square It Up
Assembly Diagram 80" x 90"

Land & Sea Bargello Place Mats

Bring harmony to your daily dining. Set the tone with these tranquil place mats.

Design by Carolyn S. Vagts for The Village Pattern Company

Skill Level
Beginner

Finished Size
Place Mat Size: 18" x 13"
Number of Mats: 2

MATERIALS

- 7–10 (2½" x 42") precut coordinating/contrasting strips
- ⅝ yard coordinating solid or tonal
- ¾ yard backing
- Batting to size
- Thread
- Basic sewing tools and supplies

CUTTING

From coordinating solid or tonal:
- Cut 3 (2½" x 42") strips.
  Subcut 4 (2½" x 14½") A strips and 4 (2½" x 13½") B strips.

- Cut 4 (2¼" x 42") binding strips.

From backing:
- Cut 2 (22" x 17") backing rectangles.

PREPARING THE BARGELLO PANEL

1. Lay out the 2½" x 42" strips on a table, making sure that there is a good contrast between them.
2. Assign each strip a number, starting at the top of the arrangement as shown in Figure 1.

Figure 1

3. Starting with strips 1 and 2, join strips in numerical order in sets of two; press seams in the same direction from strip 1 to strip 8 or from strip 8 to strip 1.

4. Join the pairs to complete the pieced panel; press seams in the same direction.

5. Subcut the strip set into the following segments in the order given: 2½", 2", 1½", 2", 2½", 3", 2½" and 2½" as shown in Figure 2. Set aside remainder of strip set for second place mat.

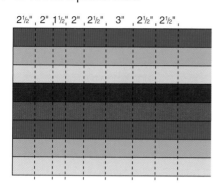

Figure 2

6. Place segments 1 and 2 right side up and move segment 2 so that the pieces in the segments are offset by about half as shown in Figure 3. Place the segments right sides together as arranged and stitch to join as shown in Figure 4; press seam open.

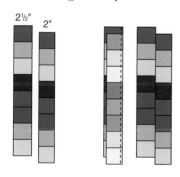

Figure 3   **Figure 4**

7. Place segment 3 next to the pieced unit and move it up or down one piece as desired to create a pattern; sew to the previously stitched unit and press seam open.

8. Continue step 7 with remaining segments in the order cut until all segments are joined into one panel as shown in Figure 5. **Note:** *You should not move any segment up or down more than one or two pieces, or it will not create a pleasing pattern.*

Figure 5

9. Trim the bargello panel to 14½" x 9½" as shown in Figure 6 to finish.

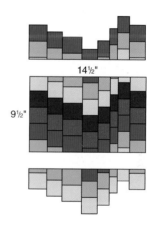

Figure 6

10. Repeat steps 5–9 to complete two bargello panels.

COMPLETING THE PLACE MATS

1. Sew an A strip to opposite long sides and B strips to opposite short ends of each bargello panel; press seams toward A and B strips to complete the two place mats.

2. Create a quilt sandwich referring to Quilting Basics on page 46.

3. Quilt as desired.

4. Bind referring to Quilting Basics on page 46 to finish. ●

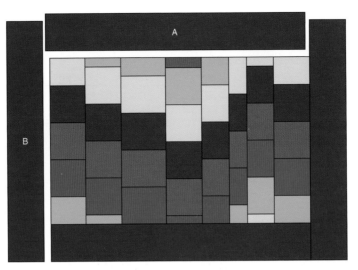

Land & Sea Bargello Place Mat
Assembly Diagram 18" x 13"

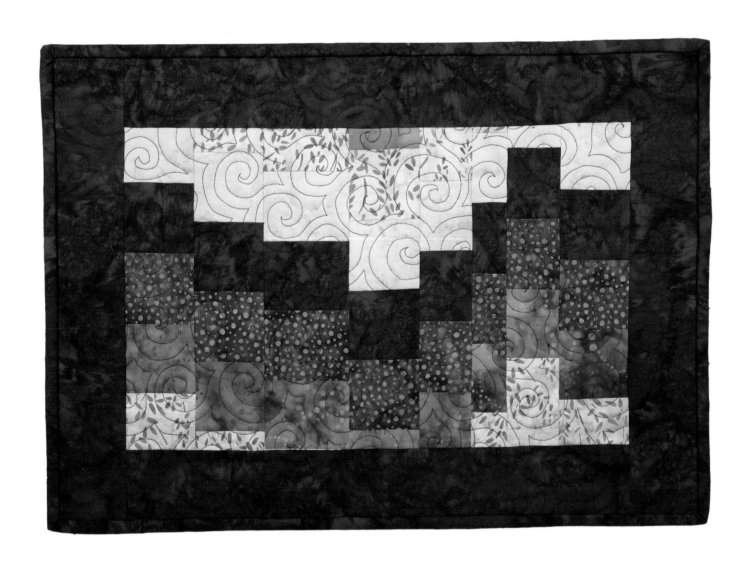

Jumpin' Jack Table Runner

Any combination of 5" squares would look wonderful in this table runner. Florals give the illusion of a garden trellis in full bloom.

Design by Gina Gempesaw

Skill Level
Beginner

Finished Size
Runner Size: 51" x 19"
Block Size: 4½" x 4½" finished
Number of Blocks: 14

MATERIALS

- 24 assorted precut 5" squares (A)
- ⅝ yard white-with-green dots
- ¾ yard dark green tonal
- Backing 59" x 27"
- Batting 59" x 27"
- Neutral-color all-purpose thread
- Quilting thread
- Basic sewing tools and supplies

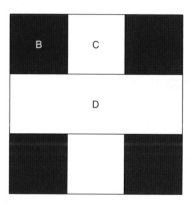

Setting Block
4½" x 4½" Finished Block
Make 14

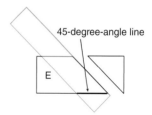

45-degree-angle line

Figure 1

CUTTING

From white-with-green dots:

- Cut 6 (2" by fabric width) strips.
  Subcut strips into 28 (2") C squares, 14 (2" x 5") D rectangles and 18 (2" x 3⅞") E rectangles. Cut one end of each E rectangle at a 45-degree angle as shown in Figure 1.

- Cut 1 (5½" by fabric width) strip.
  Subcut strip into 5 (5½") squares. Cut each square on both diagonals to make 20 F triangles; discard 2 triangles.

From dark green tonal:

- Cut 4 (2" by fabric width) strips.
  Subcut strips into 74 (2") B squares.
- Cut 5 (2¼" by fabric width) binding strips.

COMPLETING THE BLOCKS

1. To make one Setting block, select one D rectangle, two C squares and four B squares.
2. Sew a C square between two B squares to make a B-C unit as shown in Figure 2; press seams toward B. Repeat to make a second B-C unit.

Figure 2

3. Sew a D rectangle between the two B-C units to complete one Setting block referring to the block drawing; press seams away from D.
4. Repeat steps 1–3 to complete a total of 14 Setting blocks.

COMPLETING THE SIDE UNITS

1. To make one side unit, sew a B square to the square end of each E piece to make a B-E unit as shown in Figure 3; press seams toward B.

Figure 3

2. Sew a B-E unit to an F triangle to complete a side unit as shown in Figure 4; press seam away from F.

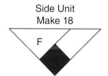

Side Unit
Make 18

Figure 4

3. Repeat steps 1 and 2 to complete a total of 18 side units.

COMPLETING THE TABLE RUNNER

1. Arrange and join the side units in diagonal rows with the Setting blocks and the A squares referring to Figure 5; press seams toward A.

Figure 5

2. Join the rows to complete the pieced top; press seams in one direction.
3. Create a quilt sandwich referring to Quilting Basics on page 46.
4. Quilt as desired.
5. Bind referring to Quilting Basics on page 46 to finish. ●

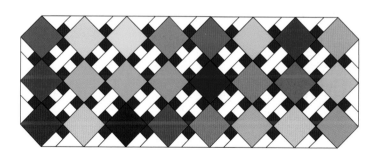

Jumpin' Jack Table Runner
Placement Diagram 51" x 19"

Quilting Basics

The following is a reference guide. For more information, consult a comprehensive quilting book.

ALWAYS:

- Read through the entire pattern before you begin your project.
- Purchase quality, 100 percent cotton fabrics.
- When considering prewashing, do so with ALL of the fabrics being used. Generally, prewashing is not required in quilting.
- Use ¼" seam allowance for all stitching unless otherwise instructed.
- Use a short-to-medium stitch length.
- Make sure your seams are accurate.

QUILTING TOOLS & SUPPLIES

- Rotary cutter and mat
- Scissors for paper and fabric
- Nonslip quilting rulers
- Marking tools
- Sewing machine
- Sewing machine feet:
- ¼" seaming foot (for piecing)
- Walking or even-feed foot (for piecing or quilting)
- Darning or free-motion foot (for free-motion quilting)
- Quilting hand-sewing needles
- Straight pins
- Curved safety pins for basting
- Seam ripper
- Iron and ironing surface

BASIC TECHNIQUES
Appliqué
FUSIBLE APPLIQUÉ

All templates are reversed for use with this technique.

1. Trace the instructed number of templates ¼" apart onto the paper side of paper-backed fusible web. Cut apart the templates, leaving a margin around each, and fuse to the wrong side of the fabric following fusible web manufacturer's instructions.
2. Cut the appliqué pieces out on the traced lines, remove paper backing and fuse to the background referring to the appliqué motif given.
3. Finish appliqué raw edges with a straight, satin, blanket, zigzag or blind-hem machine stitch with matching or invisible thread.

TURNED-EDGE APPLIQUÉ

1. Trace the printed reversed templates onto template plastic. Flip the template over and mark as the right side.
2. Position the template, right side up, on the right side of fabric and lightly trace, spacing images ½" apart. Cut apart, leaving a ¼" margin around the traced lines.
3. Clip curves and press edges ¼" to the wrong side around the appliqué shape.
4. Referring to the appliqué motif, pin or baste appliqué shapes to the background.
5. Hand-stitch shapes in place using a blind stitch and thread to match or machine-stitch using a short blind hemstitch and either matching or invisible thread.

Borders

Most patterns give an exact size to cut borders. You may check those sizes by comparing them to the horizontal and vertical center measurements of your quilt top.

STRAIGHT BORDERS

1. Mark the centers of the side borders and quilt top sides.
2. Stitch borders to quilt top sides with right sides together and matching raw edges and center marks using a ¼" seam. Press seams toward borders.
3. Repeat with top and bottom border lengths.

MITERED BORDERS

1. Add at least twice the border width to the border lengths instructed to cut.
2. Center and sew the side borders to the quilt, beginning and ending stitching ¼" from the quilt corner and backstitching (Figure 1). Repeat with the top and bottom borders.

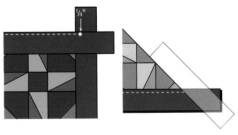

Figure 1   **Figure 2**

3. Fold and pin quilt right sides together at a 45-degree angle on one corner (Figure 2). Place a straightedge along the fold and lightly mark a line across the border ends.

4. Stitch along the line, backstitching to secure. Trim seam to ¼" and press open (Figure 3).

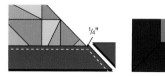

Figure 3

Quilt Backing & Batting

We suggest that you cut your backing and batting 8" larger than the finished quilt-top size. If preparing the backing from standard-width fabrics, remove the selvages and sew two or three lengths together; press seams open. If using 108"-wide fabric, trim to size on the straight grain of the fabric.

Prepare batting the same size as your backing. You can purchase prepackaged sizes or battings by the yard and trim to size.

Quilting

1. Press quilt top on both sides and trim all loose threads.
2. Make a quilt sandwich by layering the backing right side down, batting and quilt top centered right side up on flat surface and smooth out. Pin or baste layers together to hold.
3. Mark quilting design on quilt top and quilt as desired by hand or machine. **Note:** *If you are sending your quilt to a professional quilter, contact them for specifics about preparing your quilt for quilting.*
4. When quilting is complete, remove pins or basting. Trim batting and backing edges even with raw edges of quilt top.

Binding the Quilt

1. Join binding strips on short ends with diagonal seams to make one long strip; trim seams to ¼" and press seams open (Figure 4).

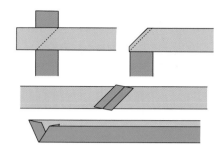

Figure 4

2. Fold 1" of one short end to wrong side and press. Fold the binding strip in half with wrong sides together along length, again referring to Figure 4; press.
3. Starting about 3" from the folded short end, sew binding to quilt top edges, matching raw edges and using a ¼" seam. Stop stitching ¼" from corner and backstitch (Figure 5).

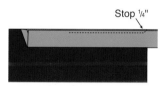

Figure 5

4. Fold binding up at a 45-degree angle to seam and then down even with quilt edges, forming a pleat at corner, referring to Figure 6.

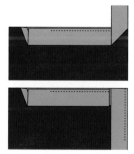

Figure 6

5. Resume stitching from corner edge as shown in Figure 6, down quilt side, backstitching ¼" from next corner. Repeat, mitering all corners, stitching to within 3" of starting point.
6. Trim binding end long enough to tuck inside starting end and complete stitching (Figure 7).

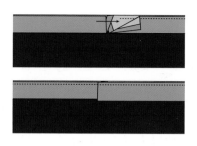

Figure 7

7. Fold binding to quilt back and stitch in place by hand or machine to complete your quilt.

QUILTING TERMS

- **Appliqué:** Adding fabric motifs to a foundation fabric by hand or machine (see Appliqué section of Basic Techniques).
- **Basting:** This temporarily secures layers of quilting materials together with safety pins, thread or a spray adhesive in preparation for quilting the layers.

  Use a long, straight stitch to hand- or machine-stitch one element to another holding the elements in place during construction and usually removed after construction.
- **Batting:** An insulating material made in a variety of fiber contents that is used between the quilt top and back to provide extra warmth and loft.
- **Binding:** A finishing strip of fabric sewn to the outer raw edges of a quilt to cover them.

  Straight-grain binding strips, cut on the crosswise straight grain of the fabric (see Straight & Bias Grain Lines illustration on the next page), are commonly used.

  Bias binding strips are cut at a 45-degree angle to the straight grain of the fabric. They are used when binding is being added to curved edges.
- **Block:** The basic quilting unit that is repeated to complete the quilt's design composition. Blocks can be pieced, appliquéd or solid and are usually square or rectangular in shape.
- **Border:** The frame of a quilt's central design used to visually complete the design and give the eye a place to rest.

- **Fabric Grain:** The fibers that run either parallel (lengthwise grain) or perpendicular (crosswise grain) to the fabric selvage are straight grain.

  Bias is any diagonal line between the lengthwise or crosswise grain. At these angles the fabric is less stable and stretches easily. The true bias of a woven fabric is a 45-degree angle between the lengthwise and crosswise grain lines.

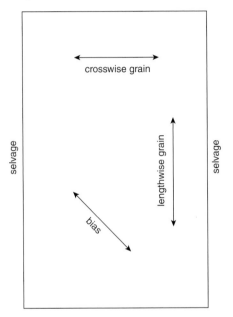

Straight & Bias Grain Lines

- **Mitered Corners:** Matching borders or turning bindings at a 45-degree angle at corners.
- **Patchwork:** A general term for the completed blocks or quilts that are made from smaller shapes sewn together.
- **Pattern:** This may refer to the design of a fabric or to the written instructions for a particular quilt design.
- **Piecing:** The act of sewing smaller pieces and/or units of a block or quilt together.

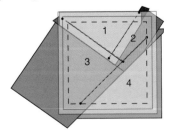

Foundation Piecing

Paper or foundation piecing is sewing fabric to a paper or cloth foundation in a certain order.

String or chain piecing is sewing pieces together in a continuous string without clipping threads between sections.

String or Chain Piecing

Pressing: Pressing is the process of placing the iron on the fabric, lifting it off the fabric and placing it down in another location to flatten seams or crease fabric without sliding the iron across the fabric.

Quilters do not usually use steam when pressing, since it can easily distort fabric shapes.

Generally, seam allowances are pressed toward the darker fabric in quilting so that they do not show through the lighter fabric.

Seams are pressed in opposite directions where seams are being joined to allow seams to butt against each other and to distribute bulk.

Seams are pressed open when multiple seams come together in one place.

If you have a question about pressing direction, consult a comprehensive quilting guide for guidance.

- **Quilt (noun):** A sandwich of two layers of fabric with a third insulating material between them that is then stitched together with the edges covered or bound.
- **Quilt (verb):** Stitching several layers of fabric materials together with a decorative design. Stippling, crosshatch, channel, in-the-ditch, free-motion, allover and meandering are all terms for quilting designs.

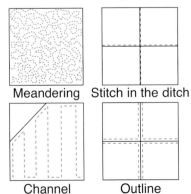

Meandering   Stitch in the ditch

Channel   Outline

- **Quilt Sandwich:** A layer of insulating material between a quilt's top and back fabric.
- **Rotary Cutting:** Using a rotary cutting blade and straightedge to cut fabric.
- **Sashing:** Strips of fabric sewn between blocks to separate or set off the designs.
- **Subcut:** A second cutting of rotary-cut strips that makes the basic shapes used in block and quilt construction.
- **Template:** A pattern made from a sturdy material which is then used to cut shapes for patchwork and appliqué quilting.

QUILTING SKILL LEVELS

- **Beginner:** A quilter who has been introduced to the basics of cutting, piecing and assembling a quilt top and is working to master these skills. Someone who has the knowledge of how to sandwich, quilt and bind a quilt, but may not have necessarily accomplished the task yet.
- **Confident Beginner:** A quilter who has pieced and assembled several quilt tops and is comfortable with the process, and is now ready to move on to more challenging techniques and projects using at least two different techniques.
- **Intermediate:** A quilter who is comfortable with most quilting techniques and has a good understanding for design, color and the whole process. A quilter who is experienced in paper piecing, bias piecing and projects involving multiple techniques. Someone who is confident in making fabric selections other than those listed in the pattern.
- **Advanced:** A quilter who is looking for a challenging design. Someone who knows she or he can make any type of quilt. Someone who has the skills to read, comprehend and complete a pattern, and is willing to take on any technique. A quilter who is comfortable in her or his skills and has the ability to select fabric suited to the project. ●